Names Above Houses

CRAB ORCHARD AWARD

SERIES IN POETRY

T0025723

NAMES
ABOVE
HOUSES

Oliver de la Paz

Crab Orchard Review

&

Southern Illinois University Press

CARBONDALE AND
EDWARDSVILLE

Copyright © 2001 by Oliver de la Paz

All rights reserved

Printed in the United States of America

13   12   11   10   7   6   5   4

The Crab Orchard Award Series in Poetry is a joint publishing venture of
Southern Illinois University Press and *Crab Orchard Review*. This series has
been made possible by the generous support of the Office of the President
of Southern Illinois University and the Office of the Vice Chancellor for
Academic Affairs and Provost at Southern Illinois University Carbondale.

Crab Orchard Award Series in Poetry Editor: Jon Tribble
Judge for 2000: Rodney Jones

Text design by Erin Kirk New

Library of Congress Cataloging-in-Publication Data

De la Paz, Oliver, [date]
Names above houses / Oliver de la Paz.
p. cm.—(Crab Orchard award series in poetry)
1. Filipino Americans—Poetry. 2. Philippines—Poetry. 3. Boys—Poetry.
I. Title. II. Series.
PS3554.E114 N36 2001   00-059495
811'.6—dc21
ISBN 0-8093-2382-6 (paper : alk. paper)

The paper used in this publication meets the minimum requirements of
American National Standard for Information Sciences—Permanence
of Paper for Printed Library Materials, ANSI Z39.48-1992. ∞

For my father. For my mother.

When a child is ready to walk,

put him on the stairs. Have him step

on a plate or anywhere else

so long as his feet do not touch the

ground first. This is to ensure that

he will always find his way

home from wherever he may roam.

—FILIPINO FOLK SAYING

Contents

THREE

Acknowledgments

Thanks to the following publications where many of the poems in this book first appeared:

The Asian Pacific American Journal—"Fidelito Suddenly Becomes Afraid of Heights"

Borderlands: Texas Poetry Review—"What Fidelito Knows of His Father"

The Clackamas Literary Review—"In the Year of the Rat," "Grounding," "Fidelito Takes Flight up a Ladder," "With the Grace of Basket Weavers"

Crab Orchard Review—"Domingo's Advice for Fidelito," "At Sea Domingo Learned to Steady His Hand"

The Cream City Review—"The Death of Domingo Recto," "Domingo's Blood Clot"

Hanging Loose—"The Fourth Madonna"

The Literary Review—"After the Boy Goes to Bed" under the title "After Fidelito Goes to Bed," "Domingo, Too Old for Fishing," "An Anatomy of Birds," "In the Dream with Blue Snow"

The Marlboro Review—"The Puzzle of Kites," "For Hours, Fidelito Hangs from the Topmost Branch Before Letting Go" under the title "For Forty-Five Hours, Fidelito Hangs from the Topmost Branch Before Letting Go"

Mockingbird—"From the Ocean, Fidelito Pulls," "Manong Jose Remembers Fidelito's First Fall"

Passages North—"The Romance of Bait"

Perihelion—"The Fisherman's Chronicle," "A Cupboard Full of Halos," "What the Laundry Told Maria Elena," "Maria Elena Puts His Good Shoes Away"

Quarterly West—"Nine Secrets the Recto Family Can't Tell the Boy," "Insects in Maria Elena's Kitchen"

Third Coast—"School Years," "Origami Dove," "Earth and Sky"

"Three Madonnas," under the title "The Family with Three Madonnas," appears in *Tilting the Continent: Southeast Asian American Literature*, edited by Shirley Goek-lin Lim and Cheng-Lok Chua.

Nick Carbó, Jeanne E. Clark , Norman Dubie, Denise Duhamel, M. Evelina Galang, Beckian Fritz-Goldberg, Rigoberto González, Susan McCabe, Bino Realuyo, Alberto Ríos, and Eileen Tabios: thank you for your advice, your support, and your friendship.

ONE

When Fidelito's first tooth fell out, his mother threw it on the roof so that the rats would find it. They were up there searching for coins. Evenings on the tin roof, their nails clicked like hail—they were always up to something: gambling, counting money. The change in his mother's jar once filled the glass to the mouth. Now she swore she had seen rats with silver disks between their teeth. Still, the old women in the village who muttered about refusing dark fruits and curing tetanus with the ends of a cephalopod, the plastic part of cuttlefish bone, said rats were lucky. They told her to throw her son's first lost tooth on the roof for them to find. When the new tooth grew in, it would be strong like the rat's.

The macaws found the tooth first. It could have been worse. His tooth might have been found by ants. Fidelito would have grown antennae and that would have presented the problem of appearances. At least you could hide wings under a shirt.

Fidelito's mother found a pair of nubs bordering his spine. They were drawn up like hands wringing their own skin from themselves, two clenched fists. Translated, it was the odd grace. A boy has no discernible nimbus, though she found him at one year to be an accomplished craftsman. All day he would gather twine from his mother's frayed skirts and braid them into wreaths of darker hues.

Fidelito's mother is picking up his nimbus again. This aura is hard to see. Quite careless for a boy of two, he leaves it where he knows someone is liable to snare a foot and fall with the splendor of an exploding green fly. That happened once to Luis the mail courier. As mail couriers go, Luis is without much seriousness and is given to moments of exaggeration. The nimbus had closed itself around his ankle, or at least that's what he says, and mail tore itself open and spread all over the village so that Eduviges Mateo learned about her husband's habit of discounting the melon prices for Florizel Francisco in exchange for marmosets. How sinister to love marmosets—the white-wigged kind. The thing is with that kind of love, there is a boy in a tree, possibly among the wigged-ones, and he is picking off leaves with his teeth because he is not accountable for that symbol he has lost. And like that, you really can't blame a man for his love of tufted ears and the long tail.

Fidelito's mother tried to trace her genealogy for the origins of wings. There was Perfecto Reyes, her brother who believed he was a macaque. Trinidad Biliboan, her great aunt, felt compelled to rescue sea-spume from the ocean. Even Dindo Pimintel, her brother-in-law, had traces of insanity. He had a relationship with geckos that the villagers could not construe as natural and had developed a system of manual suction cups for scaling the plaster of his house to sun himself with the lizards away from the tortures of shade. They had all met untimely deaths.

At two, Fidelito had grown too heavy for his atrophic nubs. When one is young, one sees so many terrible omens and has no way of knowing that the sky with its furious lie is not thicker than water. The motels rattling along the beaches, the thin sway of the coconuts never erasing their solitude. Fidelito learns to see through these as one would look through windows, embarrassed by fictions he has made about his charming looks—two, and already quite handsome. At any rate, the boy with atrophic nubs has a lot to contend with—the irregular feature of his back, the ellipse.

Appearances were getting hard to make with Fidelito. He was always climbing tamarind trees. Itong Dimaculangan, the village crazy man, would ascend after him singing the *Ave Maria* and smoking his thick cigars. Itong had a fondness for the signs of apocalypse. Cherubim-seeking took place in lofty places. And he would invoke Fidelito's name with every branch he scaled like some dramatic act of contrition.

Ascension is nothing for Fidelito. It starts with the arms hugging the base of a thick tree. Then with the knees and the feet joining in embrace. The feet and the heels searching for crevices on the skin of the tree, then the arms sliding slowly up the shaft. The feet, then the arms. Keep inching along like that until coming to a branch. But always remember to breathe. Saying your name every inch of the way is one form of exhalation. Say it. Repeat it. First the right foot, then the left. Plant them on the tree's skin so they are not free. Then bring the arms up, forming an *O* overhead; don't let go. Say it. Fidelito.

The Romance of Bait

Domingo listens to the ebb of waters, bends close to the ocean, and knows his boat must go miles past the jetty into deeper waters. He holds his jaw up to the sun, his shoulders so much like the Pacific bearing up the dome of his skull, a head drifting like a lost buoy. The air is salt. The gulls clack on the docks, waiting for fisherman to neglect their bait.

He sets two wicker pails to dangle on stiff bamboo and shoulders his crux filled with shrimp, their transparent skins. There is earth inside them. The bait merchants kept the baskets of crustaceans on the dirt floor, making each shell-curl something from a buried dream. The gulls descend like a curtain closing for evening. Domingo covers the mouths of the baskets with plastic flaps to guard the bait. The shrimp are soft and frail, like his ear listening to Maria Elena breathe in her sleep.

By holding his right arm by the wrist. And so Domingo shaves, straight razor in the right hand, his boy Fidelito at his side, the fog of the mirror settling into the harbor, and the left hand gripping tight around the right wrist. He feels as if he holds a rope to secure himself from floating away, as if he holds the arm of someone fallen overboard.

The faucet's slurred talk: a hair the drain could not swallow, the sounds of a wet deck's sway as sea-storms rock iron ships like empty plastic cups in the wind.

Fidelito's father, his eyes filled with boats and sailor's boots, steadies himself by spreading his feet wide like the stance of a man guarding a door, like a man whose balance is turned by wave-crest and spume at the hull side. The blade's prow cuts through the Pacific, past the mountains of his face like a tiller, like the furrow of his boy's forehead in surprise when Domingo cuts himself and the water in the sink blossoms.

They meet on the shelf, making music with their legs. The house fills with raptures. Scratches on the broken woodgrain are their signatures.

Beneath the house, they make their way with their hungers close to earth. They make no apologies when leaking between the floorboards. They know about the body. They move with the glow of something stolen.

The Flood of Ants

In they came to the house through spaces between floorboards, sideways rain. They ate and ate. They were brilliant like a flash in a river. They took the sugar. They poured into the bedroom, blind, maniacal. They took to the sheets. They were hideous of intent. They were naked so they crawled into Fidelito's clothes and tried to be inconspicuous in his pockets, black specks of dust. They fed and fattened themselves on food Maria Elena cooked. They gave no thanks, said no good-byes. They never left. They hung around like spice in dry air.

A Parable

A family lived in a house among ants with a door, a wall, a pile of clothes, a chair, and many fruit trees—perhaps mangos or something bright and tropical. A family living among fruits and ants is not a happy family for long.

On weekends, the ant king with fierce mandibles knocked with his crown. The family stood near the door. One family member stayed seated in the chair, since the wall needed no bearing up, despite the noise from pincers or the strum of ant feet.

Of course, the fruit king could bear none of this and took all his possessions away from the family, being sensitive, easily bruised.

Then the armies of the ant king stormed the house, seeking the fruit king, though he had since gone.

At night the family listened to the static of legs marching through the door.

The next morning, a basket of oranges appeared in front of the door from a lover of the fruit king. Sick of it all, the chair toppled over. The wall crumbled. The family stepped outside, not by choice, but as a result of oranges. While gathering a pile of clothes and oranges, the family thought, never set house among the ants and the fruits.

In the distance they heard jaws click like castanets.

Before Takeoff, Fidelito Prays

Let us sing of what can be carried.
Let our songs be of hand-carry and Balikbayan boxes.

Let us praise stamps and tickets for passage. Let us sing
The song of duct tape and markers, the song of twine and cardboard.

Let our songs be of shelter for family and pictures.
Let us praise pictures of family picnics and singing

And arms holding children. Let us forget
Humid days left behind and the green, the green . . .

Let children make shelter on plane seats. Let us hide
From the stewardess and no one else.

Let tickets repeat our names and end
Our voices of constant worry. Let us separate

Name from name, mother from mother. Let us praise
An end to ants and hands covering mouths.

Let our worries be of constant singing. Praise our worry.
Let our singing be constant passage.

For children are passing constantly. Praise our passage.
Let the roar of the plane shelter us from worry.

Praise these engines that bring us passage.
Praise our mouths, our constant singing . . .

Below, farmers make crosshairs of their hoes. Untended crops grow
jealous of the boy marking the rows with his shadow, irretrievable X.

Then clouds roll in. Some hint of regret coasts when birds leave.
Empty, the trees fade, dark and yawning.

Fidelito, now out of sight, delivers his name to thunderheads in black
shoes. Such are the formalities with rain.

The fasten-seat-belt light flashes and the boy, pressing his hands to the walls, locks himself in the bathroom cubicle, draws his knees up to his chest with his arms, and squeezes his body into a ball.

He misses so much. When he turns on the faucet to drown the sounds of the engine, he passes Guam. When the diaper-changing board falls on his head, he's missed Hawaii. The mouths of volcanoes jaw at the plane as it passes while the bags in the overhead bins huddle together.

Fidelito Haunts Airports

In the way plastic bags in shopping carts fix to one wheel, Fidelito wanders through the terminal with his mother, Maria Elena. He leans on windows, presses his palms to the glass, and stares at the engines' eyes, the way they blur the air with their gaze.

His mother drags him by his belt to the baggage claim. Once there, Fidelito sits on the black conveyor belt, goes under the tunnel's black rubber entrance flap, and says hello to the men on the other side. They are surprised.

Fidelito, a boy among suitcases and boxes, chugs along until bright lights spiral and alarms squawk telling him it's time to get off.

On the other side, the newly arrived scan the mouth of the carousel, separated from things they will carry into their houses. Maria Elena waits for her parcel: a disheveled boy clutching a blue suitcase bearing his name.

Fidelito walks backwards. The black rubber rails gleam beneath his palms like pythons. Never mind the travelers who want to go down steps pouring from the grate's metal teeth, that there are places they need to be—

The mechanical whine, a song in Fidelito's skull. It guides his legs to climb up when the world goes down. Now a line of people ready to descend to their baggage wait at the top of the escalator. Fidelito, going nowhere, edges closer to, then farther from firm ground. He casts his eyes downward, knowing when he stops, it will be much further to climb.

Manong Jose, While Cleaning His Last Window Before Coffee, Sees Fidelito and Is Pleased Though Wary

They've come off the plane like so many spent and dirty rags I've used on airport windows, split, threadbare and dim. But it's good to see folks from the old country. She with her three hand-carry bags, probably all she owns. He with the look of a bruised warrior, or a man unsure of his footstep after being set adrift too long. Then there's the boy.

That kid there is a rough one. He looks beautiful and misunderstood like martyrs. All aura and golden, though pierced with the spit of the faithless. Yes, he's a rough one who carries himself with too much purpose for a child his age. I feel the pull of the moon in him. It's in the way he wears his hair, the cowlick up, forever ascending . . .

Fidelito Prays to the Wind, Asking for Advice, but Not Really Asking

Of all the signs in the world,
The wind, pausing for a second,
Is my colored dream . . . blues and rouges.
I see its aches are final and sad.
If I were up there, the wind would know
What to do with my arms.
I might talk to it and smooth back
The hair from its forehead
The way mother does for me. If I were
Up there, I would begin my study of the earth.
I am here too early in the year
With the nag of my misplaced wings,
Here before birds awaken—
With this sadness over a small thing.

TWO

They last long for Fidelito, who is not of this earth. With its alphabets and loose-leaf, sheets of construction paper, oranges, blues, lunch boxes, crepe paper, papier-mâché, the teacher talk and rasp of chalk, long division, multiplication, pronunciation, spelling and quelled hungers at lunch hour, the recesses of chase the girls/boys catch-as-catch-can, freeze tag, war with rubber balls and big red welts the size of baseballs, war with a deck of cards, war of pencil breaking, or tether ball, kick ball, being goof balls in back near the coat racks, learning to cuss and whistle at the same time, saying Jesus, Mary, Joseph, holy, holy, holy . . . Lord, the girls who dare each other to kiss Fidelito, as he sits in the corner, dazed, watching birds in the frozen light.

He is a frequent eclipse . . . a shadow on fire. The light breaks over the schoolyard and a hallucination of evenly cropped trees in stride moves the glass. As the dark forms of spruce pass his face, he disappears.

He keeps his mouth shut and his palms open despite the steady drum of spit-wads, kid-song, and the long clock's nervous face. Bells refuse to breathe. And the wide hours wait for doors to open.

Fidelito gazes outside. There are other milder distractions: some of the children eat their shirts and some burst into rain. A road burns into a corner. In the power lines above the playground, a grackle's steel eye murders the earth. And the sky, now perfect for flight, is open like the older mouth of our moon.

Why Maria Elena Calls the Boy's Name So Many Times in a Day

Because any minute it will rain—because skylines are false. Because
there's always sparrow's dust in his hair, bark-colored. Because that scrap
of her voice makes the boy sway in place like a dangled chain. Because
the neighbor's dog is in the garden again, always in the garden. Because
when the boy plays, the neighbors emerge from their houses like they're
listening for a sound, their ears pressed groundward. Because a boy
in a storm grays the hair of a mother, while a sad necklace sways from
her throat.

A blur of upwardness that is climbing. The flat board pressed to palm, pressed to foot sole. It becomes motion—slurred arrival, which Fidelito makes: first step, second step. The ladder stretches like an awkward smile of hello, of departure.

The boy, trusting only what he feels by hand, begins to forget the ground. With his right foot on the first rung, he hears the sky call his name. When the left meets the right, he hears birdcall. Then the horizon moves on without him. Then the last board before the fall. When the right and left are reconciled, Fidelito finds himself unsteady, his legs paired as if bound. A pause. Nowhere left to go.

Meanwhile, in the blue above, larks explode like hours following hours.

For Hours, Fidelito Hangs from the Topmost Branch
Before Letting Go

Because, after rain, it smells like green tea his mother brews on slow
mornings, because he likes the view of the world upside down from this
height, he hooks his legs around the topmost branch of the world's sixth-
largest Douglas fir. Fidelito has a mission. There is a certain grace with
trees, he thinks, and hanging from one for a long time will show him how
little he needs his legs, whether his dreams are different, whether he is
closer, the way mountains or skyscrapers or even Douglas firs scratch the
back of the sky.

If Fidelito is part of the order of back-scratchers he will know simply by
hanging around until slowly his blood, in an act of defiance, rouses itself
from his feet and leaves in procession down the arteries of his knees,
marching, red ants renewing their contract with gravity, and dizzy,
Fidelito lets go.

In the sink where the grease rainbows bloom. They overflow like neon in cities of rain. She hears her name again, called above noises of the house.

Again the wrens are in the garden, their white throats ghosting around the boy fallen from a birch in the yard. The mother, hands still damp, kneels and holds her boy's broken wrist. She feels his unsteady pulse and shields her one-winged son. All around, the mouths chit syllables: an aphasic's name, an angel's stammer . . .

Again the tree, heavy with birds, moves like a lung.

Fidelito Suddenly Becomes Afraid of Heights

When Fidelito starts across the Golden Gate Bridge, he only gets halfway
before cars stutter, the way flanks of huddled gazelles twitch when
spooked by lions, the cables sway to the wind gusts blown from Oakland,
and girder-groan-shudder makes the mind of the dizzy boy feel itself spill
into the harbor where seals below blow bubbles and croak at Fidelito,
knock-kneed, hunkering down, unsteady—

If only his bones were built from the same stuff as this rust-orange bridge,
if only seals weren't so noisy, if only traffic would flow more slowly, evenly.
If, only.

From the Ocean, Fidelito Pulls

A dull starfish, one with six arms. It's hard like limpet shells on salty rocks and burns its tan heart. Underneath, the feelers search the way the blind cling to the walls of a hall. Its beak mouths at the air for speech while Fidelito hangs to one of its arms curling like a child's finger. The starfish waves that way.

Far out at sea, the long boat of Fidelito's father sighs, a blue flame on the horizon. In his yellow slicker, Domingo tugs at his net and pulls up more stars. They give themselves from the ocean.

Domingo hears bells on a red buoy clang in rhythm. On the prow, he spreads his legs apart to steady himself, the horizon dipping and rising before him. Then he sits and sleeps. The nets drag their brash hairs in the wake.

A sea marker rings, urgent and secret, as a gull nests on its perch. It is this way for hours: only two voices. Soon the gull goes looking for the sky. Domingo, snoring in indigo, disappears as the sun sets.

Far away, the harbor lights close like a sequined hand.

Grounding

At noon the cloud-plume's whorled face divides the sky, weather unstable
for flight. So Fidelito, sullen and gray, fills a stiff chair by the window and
sulks like a salty rag. Swimming, water streaks the glass . . .

Fidelito, looking out angrily, admires stars. They can't resist drawing
their wings back inside the storm's mouth. He wonders—what now that
winds pull the hair of trees? Then the rain. Its hollow fingers strum against
the roof.

Poor Fidelito. How children drown in the language of thundershowers.
Now, he thinks, mockery is being made of him, grounded. The rain gutters
pool long necklaces of sound, making asphalt gleam. Somewhere, Fidelito
thinks, the stars and their shrouded eyes peer into his dry house.

Those reports of death when you fall in dreams are untrue. Fidelito
falls constantly, even in sleep. In dark he is the jolt—blue pajamas that
streak through night. It is mean travel in dreamtime—his two-foot drop
lasting hours.

He soars by a building shaped like a party hat, the harbor not far from
view. The sun from its black-mirrored windows hits his eyes and he drops
twenty stories. The impossible blue cars below breathe their solitudes and
grow larger. All the while his arms twitch the way a horse does with
nervousness.

And like a bright glare in Fidelito's eyes, there is confusion. In his sleep,
a wing flap sounds like fish riding away in the bay or the whisper of colts
munching tufts of grasses. From this, he is helpless lying down.

Three Madonnas

The first Madonna's languid arm gleams from television light. Tired in her blue robe, she sees on-screen lovers kiss, like the snooze of boats drifting past. Through the snow of the cathode, snores of a man on the sofa, alone. It is raining and the roar of the tube turned furnace makes the Madonna dream. Outside, the porch light kills the sky while birches burn with fireflies trembling through a storm.

The second Madonna, stern on the dash of the car, lifts her eyes to the rearview mirror when Maria Elena puts it in reverse. She stands, hands folded like a mast, and frowns at the cars in repose.

Some of the drivers stare straight ahead, listening to invisible trees. Look there, through the windshield—the cry of a disintegrating star.

The third Madonna holds cracks in her porcelain hands. She rests in the closet next to a pair of sneakers. There are reasonable coats hung like gentlemen. They spill into the dark, strangers . . . like the one just stepped off a train wearing a white camellia in his lapel. Through the glass as the train steams by damp houses, a woman with a blue hat dreams in roses.

She's a statuette the size of a child's thumb. The boy thinks she speaks to him. Fidelito hides her from the television's aquarium light, fearing that she may drown the way Domingo sinks below the surface of the cathode.

She appears in the bathroom on top of the toilet's water tank to prove that she's holy, unafraid.

She has been washed in Fidelito's pant-pocket four times. A miracle that her paint has not chipped.

She has appeared in wars with other statuettes her same size. The green army men freeze, toppling over when they see her.

At night she swings from a string hung from the ceiling of the boy's room, circling with the propeller blade of the ceiling fan. She blesses the room with her blue arcs.

Maria Elena thought she had left her troubles with the armored ones in another country. But they are here, crouched between boards of the side porch among viny undergrowth. Whole legions of them. So Maria Elena guards the door, various cracks in the house, drafty windows.

The world is no longer her own. A sudden ring of the phone goes unanswered for fear of invasion. Poisons sprinkled around the house curl about the rooms like an embarrassed nude. But they don't work. So, prompted by memory, Maria Elena opens every door. She prays the old prayers and watches them drift with the fumes about the house. The television fills the air with rain.

The ants are prepared. Underneath, where the boards touch ground, they churn up earth. They sing songs for wood. They lay blueprints before their armies. They celebrate blight and dying, wedged into the grains of two-by-fours like a blood clot, like a clump in the brain.

This is the house she wanted, the dark porch, the faux-marble, faux-oak, the clothes swaying on the line. She watches Domingo from the window in the yard, sitting on a lawn chair yawning in the hours. In times like these, she remembers the drum of the rain on a corrugated-tin roof and the bleat of jeepneys wheeling through the tight corners of narrow streets. In times like these, the sweet hint of pork knuckles cooking in a stew brings back ghosts from the streets of her childhood. Back, where the call of a single name sends one million white blouses to chores, emptying the streets of skirts while the boys, scabbed and blackened in their play, lose themselves to the deep onion-light.

After he fills the junk drawer in the kitchen with wreaths made from
scraps of paper, cloth, and sticks, Fidelito stores new ones in a cupboard
above the stove.

He drags a stool from the garage and sets it to reach the place where Maria
Elena keeps cookbooks. *In* the multi-hued halos go, forced. Some of them
tumble out like hula-hoops onto linoleum. Others become bracelets and
slide down his arms as he reaches up to stop them.

When he closes the door, Fidelito forgets until his mother, ready to cook,
opens the cupboard. They spill to her from the dark, a noise of coins from
another world.

The music of the tin roof, and the click of bird claws. The sheen of a rooster's wing like steel. In the dark, the wet fishing nets gleam from the light of the kerosene lamps.

Fidelito's held close, looking out the window at a man dressed in white, yoked by a stick balancing two silver buckets, drifting through the pre-dawn streets on bright operatic wings.

Hangs his net from the tallest tree in the backyard, much to the neighbors' dismay. All night, wing sounds and the sad cries of trapped birds resound—

The ground turns a bleached white from droppings. There is no escape from the smell. Even Fidelito, stuck in the net, wants to come down because of the unbreakable stench.

For weeks flocks rule the neighborhood, until Domingo, tired from noise and sleepless nights, cuts the tangled ends of the net. The black-winged mass of the net rises, begins to fly southward.

Fidelito, without his father knowing it, is woven in with the birds. He hangs to a corner of the flock-quilt and dangles far above his town.

Each night a new lover on screen. Each night the erotics of travel:
the Moulin Rouge, the low-cut dress of a dancer. Each night the dream
of a tuxedo and parquet floors, the heeled foot on the waxed board.
Sometimes a negligee on a lamp. Sometimes rejected dresses on the floor.
Sometimes a meager arm. Sometimes the admiring script of a letter. Like
when Domingo, looking out the window of an airplane years ago saw
the landscape of America and thought it to be handwriting, the rivers
bending in the cursive of a shaky hand.

He means it. He wants to catch the streetlights' halos stretching onward. The glow spells his name.

Fidelito makes preparations: apples in the curl of his shirt. The murmur of his father's television covers his footfall.

Here he pauses to watch the moonlike glow. On screen the uninterrupted snow of the nothing channel animates Fidelito's movement, making the shadow of his arms large enough to hold the room. And like a dark suit he stops, folds his legs beneath him, and watches the blue light on his shirt. Outside, dew on the lawn blinks like anonymous stars.

So you want to levitate, to float in the sky the way the tops of trees jut out?
Wind-stunned sparrows will nibble your earlobe. Bees will make a hive of
your hair. In rain you'll be so high no roof can cover your head. You will
fear music from brassy instruments because their notes sit in your brain
with no one to sing along. Listen, listen.

There, in that gray cloud is the woman like you. She sits lotus style and
sails like a box kite. How wonderful when she blows away, past exotic
ports near the ocean. The air eats its way through her shirt. See how the
sky darkens? She fades from sight like an uncontrollable star. But soon,
son, she will miss finer things: chairs and beds. Look, over your shoulder.
Smaller than a thumbprint, she sighs apologies. I'm sorry, she says,
I'm sorry.

Foolish, hard-headed girl. She's hovered just out of reach. You act like
that and you'll bid farewell to the ground, who is less forgiving than
your mother.

The Mole of Maria Elena's Armpit
Roughly the size of a quarter. Her husband calls it her beautiful armpit.
Once with Domingo, she wore a sleeveless shirt to the grocery store—just
once. Before patrons could stare at her as she reached for a can of peas, he
slid a hand under her arm. Now she has two wardrobes: "Public" and
"Private."

Love Postcards
There are three of them. When Domingo is away he's not one for words.
On the back of a portrait of the Columbia River, it reads, "Gone Fishing."
The self-critical one from Seattle reads, "I've just realized how much I hate
the weather here and it saddens me." The insightful third: a buxom blonde
sends greetings from Venice Beach with Domingo's note, "You can't live
here without wheels."

Overheard Long-Distance Phone Conversation
"You mean you can't distinguish between a lychee and a longan?" Cost:
six dollars.

The Boy's Ears
They think Fidelito gets them from great grandfather Carlos on Maria
Elena's side, the way they stick out like an awning. He was the talk of the
barrio then. On hot days, people paid him to turn circles and circulate the
air. Saturday nights, the people would say, "Meet you under Carlos," and
huddle under his earlobe. Often, they used him to eavesdrop on
conversations. At one point, he was the most hated man in Luzon.

The Pearls
They're glass, of course. Domingo was poor. Maria Elena with a pencil
sometimes runs the eraser-end along the grooves while her husband sits in
front of the television. It distracts him. He thinks she's unzipping the back
of her dress and chopping onions in the nude.

The Inherited Autographed Photo

It's of Sophia Loren in her younger days, playing her role as Dulcinea.
Domingo keeps it locked away in a safety deposit box at the bank. Her
hair, tied back, wants to roam. The red dress she clutches twirls into the
script of her "Sophia." When he thinks of her, Domingo hums in adagio.

The Bag of Soil

It was from under the house where Maria Elena was born. She and her
husband also lived there until the boy was born. She keeps it in her
stocking and underwear drawer. The corpses of three ants float in and out
when she shakes the bag. She thinks, when she dies, this shall be the first
earth thrown on her casket.

The Matchbook

A reminder that Domingo quit smoking when Fidelito was born. Now,
in every restaurant or hotel, he seeks them. One matchbook has a picture
of Aurora Diamond on the inside flap, a one-time headliner for the
Topless Girls of Glitter Gulch. He keeps it apart from the others. On the
cover, a blue boot moves when tilted, and the small print says "Keep your
spurs on, cowboy."

A Night on the Town

Some Saturday evenings, they leave Fidelito at home with the babysitter.
He does not hear where his parents are going, despite the largeness of his
ears. Domingo makes reservations for dinner with Maria Elena at a
seafood restaurant along the wharf. She wears her white "Private" labeled
spaghetti-strap dress, and faux-pearls. Her hair tightly braided in a long
black rope drapes over her shoulder, covering her armpit. Domingo drives
with the window rolled down and puffs away at a Cremosa lit by Aurora
Diamond. They descend on the Embarcadero to soft operetta. And in the
moonlight, the smell of the ocean and stars.

Fidelito, at his school desk, secretly folds paper into a gift. The steady scale of Fidelito's fingernail as it glides down paper to make a new edge, the sound when bathers kneel in shallows.

Fidelito stifles the crinkle as the beak he makes bends in thirst. It wants to drink like the schoolchildren in their rows who press their backs to wooden desks and bend their necks the way swans do, watching themselves drift away.

Now the folded bird wants to fly. It beats its white heart in Fidelito's restless hands.

A chalk scrawled alphabet creeps like peeling wallpaper.

Something spoken goes unheard, the way a crooked line in a signature spells boredom or a note tucked under the body of an origami dove reads desire. Messages sail into air and Fidelito, with his right hand cupped to his ear, moves forward into that sound. He hopes to catch that one dry voice in a choir of something small enough to sit in his palm.

Manong Jose Remembers Fidelito's First Fall

He thinks he's some sort of macaw standing on his roof, black and miraculous in his overcoat, always casing the sky.

Years ago, he thought a young birch was a good climbing tree. Fidelito, while trying to climb one with weak branches, felt a high limb crack. The kid flew twelve feet from roof edge, sucking up space between his face and the ground so fast he became a single column of arms, legs, and hair.

Now there's something about his body when he slouches. It's like the way you walk about when you brace yourself for a sadness without cause.

Now I see he scans the periphery of trees, especially for thick ones with large palmate leaves. He thinks the young ones are cruel, the way they explode completely like that in air.

Fidelito Contemplates How Powerful He Has Become and Thinks of Ways to Alter Weather Patterns

See how my thumb spreads the clouds?
It is simple. My arm moves the white ocean.
Flight is just that. Easy sleep—like nodding
In class to the teacher's constant talk.
That kind of rest comes only when children
Press their tongues to the desks.
I am not one for this space . . .
After school I make a blot with my thumb
And watch it grow there in the blue,
A space filling out.
The clouds pull back their hairs
And extend the arms I give them
When I close one eyelid,
Press my thumb to the sky.

THREE

Mind-Swimming

A stroke is like that, according to Domingo. Pulling up on nets, he suddenly felt heavy. Close attention to things make them strange. He felt his leg disappear. He could smell ink from newspapers. He could hear the flint struck in a lighter miles away. And like that quick strike of a flame, Domingo fell to the deck of the boat, watching the horizon before him open like the widening pupil of an eye.

After the Boy Goes to Bed

Maria Elena watches her husband disappear into the sofa like coins.
His eyes, the hard shadow of yesterday. They love each other the way old
houses lean into the sea. Not his eyes, but the gleam between woman and
man, their two bodies, the press of a knucklebone, the soft hand resting on
a knee—the way the brass in the kitchen lingers long after . . .

There is still the thoughtless rattle between them. The ink stamp stain of a
touched wrist. Maria Elena and Domingo. Their hands clasp together as
they watch their rings turn blonder in the glow of the moon.

Outside the fog rolls in. It is like pressure applied to an artery, the thick of it.

Then the sound of a car dragging its muffler up the street. Spark of asphalt and metal the way the sky over the sea lights up during a storm.

He remembers a particular squall. How he and the boat were lifted from the ocean, airborne. That feeling of nothing—the loss of contact between boot and board, wood and water.

Now Domingo is unsure of his hand on his knee. Thin blood. The left leg quite numb. As if a loved one demanded to be touched.

Sometimes, beneath the covers, it tickles Domingo. When he enters the bathroom, he thinks he feels the cold tile caress his former foot. When it is about to rain, he feels his former knee complain. There are times when he is alone that he talks to the ghost of his leg. There are times when it answers back, like when a man opens his closet for his favorite suit and a long strand of an old lover's hair rests on the sleeve.

First it starts with the eyes to spare the man from witnessing his own vanishing. He would not believe it if he saw it. Then the hearing goes. This ensures that he does not hear his own groans, the complaint of the loved one telling him he's left his foot by the door. Then the memory recedes. The man cannot remember his foot or ever having a foot. The man does not remember seeing it attached, despite the failure of his vision. The man cannot recall hearing the floorboards creak beneath his weight. This makes the man sad, though he can't remember the cause of his sorrow. And so it goes . . . and so it goes.

The Audubon show flickers like a candle when winds blow on the antennae. Birds are on the screen again. It's late. Soon the room fills with snow as local channels wave their flags. Goodnight.

The television, an aquarium glass, departs into noise. Domingo snoozes. Twitching in his sleep, he sees fleets of sloops sail away, as if torn from him. These exaggerated clouds move from the harbor and bleed into one another.

When they blossom into doves, he is not surprised. He hears the wing-flap: the sound a ship makes when it becomes a child in a white cloak, bathing.

Domingo's lips purse as he snores, whistling birdsong—sleep, pure sleep.

And in his dream he fell in love with the white wing of a bird stuck in stone in the middle of the sea. There was no background for this, no history, for example. There were no other voices, no sound from the television, no garrulous water lapping at the shore. There was no monologue of earth, no holy holy from Fidelito. No jazz band or seraphim. No Mona Lisa or rain pounding shells into sand. We could examine the evidence. A man's brain slowly filling with water. The television's aquarium light. We could say his sleep with his one hand over his head cut blood to his brain. We could, but it is no good to make such noise. No good to interrupt. No good to speculate. There was simply a dream which occurred during a man's last sleep. And in his dreaming, there was a wing, a stone, the sea, and the end.

What Fidelito Knows of His Father

Domingo Recto's head was the sun
On the shoulders of the Pacific,
A stone shorn by riptide,
A buoy on the curl of a great breaker.

His eyes took in the sea
Like green anemones, took in
The sea like the curve of a dune,
An archipelago torn by tsunami.

His nostrils were bellows,
Swirl of a whirlpool,
His nostrils were full sails.

When Domingo spoke, his lips
Curled thunderheads, when he spoke,
His lips the wash of spume on sand,
The shawls of whitecaps tossed by wind.

His chest the weight of a galleon,
The weight of a piano crate lost
At sea, chest like a rusted junk
Full of drunks far from shore.

His arms the shafts of shovels, arms
Like rails along decks that keep
Sailors from sea, his arms were knotted
Ropes holding a tattered sail.

Domingo's hands were cracked clay
Jars holding rain, a flour sack
On top of a mast, purple sea urchins
Opened by otters.

His fingers were like oarlocks,
Domingo's fingers were tossed
Branches on wave crests,
Palm fronds rocked from treetops.

Domingo Recto had a waist
Like the steerage of a slave ship,
A waist like the husk of an abalone,
Five cannons aimed at shore.

His left leg, crippled
In a shipping accident, his one
Good leg was the pivot of a compass,
His one leg, the star that points
True north, the one skid of a Catamaran,
Domingo's left leg was the tail of an eel.

His right leg, the odd dwarf of a family,
A tree trying to root on sand,
A life raft with no survivors,
Domingo's right leg was a sailor's log
With missing pages.

This is what I know of my father,
The chronicle of sea and salt leeched
Through his skin, the eye
That looks through me
As through an oncoming wave.
I was the blue-lighted
Horizon that pulled him not to land,
But to the slight curve of the ocean.

After the death of Domingo Recto, his shoes by the door wait to go outside. They know his bare feet are cold. The cracked leather tips shift their weight. The left's worn inside edge, a plow. The rubber sole of the right, smooth at the toe. His shoes tear earth with their paces. They don't rest. Listen—they leave tracks in soil.

Because of footfall, Maria Elena can't sleep. In the kitchen, the tacky sound of gum on tile, the squeak of rubber down halls, the thud of mud track.

They are the shoes of the dead. Know that by their tongues. The laces drag, limp hairs of ghosts. Fidelito hears them too, and it frightens him. In life it was Domingo's footstep to tuck him into bed, floorboards groaned from the man heavy with years. And now those shoes walk by themselves . . .

When Fidelito tried them on he stumbled, his gait too small. Only one person could move those shoes, passing in the night with open mouths.

Maria Elena puts them in the closet to forget, only to find them huddled at the foot of her bed by dawn. She is hopeless from the garments of the dead. They find ways into her sight. If Maria Elena were to give them to a bare-footed stranger, one day when on an errand, she is sure she would see them down some alleyway. Hear them hop up the street to greet her like a savage bird—

Somewhere Domingo trudges, unshod. And the ground before him is misstep. She sees the shape of the loafers by the door in the weird light of a candle and wonders whether Domingo knows which way dust floats on a worn path or if there are simple eulogies for his shoes which outlast him.

An even exchange: love for Vidalia onions, a faucet with the gleam of a pheasant's tail, a movement up and down the music of steam, the extremes of ant hungers and the blackened toast left on linoleum. Fair trade. Again the window spiked with the mouths of rain deepens her reflection. If she had been someone else—someone named Eustacia. With a name like that she could meet strangers on a train, perhaps dance on stiletto heels with chromium tips, become a storm in a red dress. If she were a red dress. If she were a train. If the hum of the refrigerator were an etude played on a white piano . . . If she were a white window from years ago . . .

For years on end the family keeps the shirts of Domingo tucked away in an armoire. Sundays, the boy sits nearby, watching for a sign. Fidelito's frail voice recites from the Book of Job, mentioning that the crossroads will be treacherous. The child does not shed a tear.

There are other precautions: If it's nice weather, he opens the windows wide. If there's rain, he sits by the glass, buttoned up tight, watching the tremor on the horizon. He checks the position he sleeps in before the dreams. He dons the dress shirt of his father like a vestment and watches a clock tick down the hours.

Fidelito is a small thing, but exaggerates his size by putting on his father's dress shirt backwards. Arm holes empty, the sleeves hang like limp wings. Fidelito steps outside in the fall air and runs fast, observing the sun following.

The shadows of skeletal trees merge with the earth to become the suspension of breath. Fidelito runs that way, feverish, sad, and armless. His mother calls. The table lamp is lit with a day's light film of dirt from the air. Only when he feels his body letting go from exhaustion does he stop. Fidelito likes being somewhere in-between, the way water evaporates, or when in the cold air, smoke forms before his mouth.

Whatever the starlings had, Fidelito caught it.

Now, sleepwalking, Fidelito senses sea-speech in rain. He slips into his catastrophe clothing—a plastic twenty-five-cent whistle between his lips, the heavy night-shirt he wears.

The call of fat drops, the thrum of water on the roof summons dreams. Eyes thick with sleep, he watches plumes of storm gather, a large bird with arms that pulls feathers of atmosphere into its body.

The moon's loud face exploding behind the cumulonimbus, the earth's tongue raked by tail feathers of this gray hawk, the surfaces of bodies of water—all come to this moment: in his baggy shirt, life vest, and whistle-in-the-mouth, Fidelito ascends the crumbling trellis outside his house. Sleepy, on his roof, he hears the tragedy in storms. He flails his arms wildly.

For squirming, Fidelito receives a pinch from his mother. Disturbed by his yowl, the once quiet congregation sing their *Aves* an octave louder.

The boy, uncomfortable under the gaze of Saint Francis de Sales who writes reports on his misbehavior, rubs a welt the size of a nickel on his arm. The hands of Thomas Aquinas, folded in prayer, frighten him too. He thinks, if he turns his head, the fingers will spring to life and pinch his ear. Briefly, Fidelito behaves.

But when the time comes to kneel and the padded boards come down from their hinges, Fidelito straddles one as though it were a horse. He urges it to run far from the stream of the Saints' blue shadows. Those praying around him bow their heads and smile.

A yoke of intersecting sticks and twine keeps Fidelito and a black kite from losing each other. Because Fidelito is always losing things, in flight the kite holds onto him, rattles as breezes kick its plastic arms. String wrapped around the knuckles of Fidelito's right hand tightens. Heels into the ground, he feels it pull him from earth. A quick tug of the line rights the path, but soon the cross nosedives. He gets the best of his shadow today. Last hours are spent breathing life into its useless limbs after the fall. The kite, in its strange sleep, coughs lightly. When the breeze has finished its last ovation, Fidelito turns to go home. String wrapped around his ankles, the kite trails, an abyss, drags itself on its belly.

When Fidelito should be sleeping, he instead pulls from under his bed a flashlight and a blue box holding cards with names of constellations. They glitter when held to light, pinholes poked through cardboard to match the sky's geography. Fidelito, mouth opened wide, holds the butt of the flashlight between his teeth. Over the narrow beam, he projects Orion on the ceiling.

Above, the dust motes spiral in the light: Sirius, Arcturus, Capella. He points at a bright blossom in the mica and tries to say its name. The glow of streetlamps bleed into the galaxy of his room. And on the pavement after rain, the headlights of a lone car fade in the bright glint of quartz trapped in asphalt. The driver, looking out his side window, sees three stars from Orion's belt lifting the boy's ceiling to the sky.

What the Laundry Told Maria Elena

Maria Elena's hands are cloth, the silk feel of foam-caked garments from washing the whites in a big basin. There are spots she agonizes over—the one with blood from her boy's first flight, grass stains on the knees of his jeans from prayer or a stumble.

She remembers her son, Fidelito, always wandering beneath the constellations' steady teeth. Now the mouths of his pant legs open with weightlessness, as if coming up for breath, as if flying among the soapy clouds, and she prays: Let me be done with this load. Let drowned clothes stay drowned so long as they come out clean. Let stains speak no more of what they saw of sky and of the fall.

Fidelito hears their song and grows angry. Wings swallow his yard squabbling over leaves.

So the boy, jealous, lugs armloads of branches into the house all day. By watching the industry of wrens, he learns to weave twigs into a wooden basket large enough to hold a crouched boy.

When he's ready, he returns to the yard and climbs. Up he goes, the bowl strapped to his back, higher, into the top of the tallest tree in the neighborhood.

The birds look on and chit, amused.

In the thickest niche where large branches join the trunk, he sets his perch and stays there even when the stars grow uncountable. He shouts above chirps and mating calls.

Finally, neighbors, angrier than he, call the fire department to get him down.

Then the ladder comes and the red lights spiral. Fidelito, sly and smiling, shakes the branches before descending.

A bird flies into Fidelito's window—the cracked glass, a spider's web.
Lying in the grass, its heart beats like a spitfire, then stops. To get the secret
of flight, he studies the rows of the corpse's wings for hours: how the
tapered form holds weight when in the air, or how the tail sticks upward
like a rudder. He even notes the way its breastbone pushes outward as if
someone had punched the bird in the stomach. Fidelito tilts his head to
imitate the sinuous neck of the bird's awkward death.

After hours of study, he makes a human-sized replica of a sparrow's wing
from construction paper. He tapes them to his arms, sticks his chest out,
raises his buttocks, flaps, and struts around like that—his head arched so
far he cannot see the ground.

There were sightings. In a bakery, a miracle handprint, roughly the size of Fidelito's, was found in the chocolate icing of a neighbor's birthday cake. Children thought they saw rain streak the glass of school windows, forming his image.

A catalogue of other signs: feathers appearing in the desks of his classmates; the swings swaying by themselves; smudges on the stained glass near the top of the ceiling—too far to reach; and his father's old clothes seen hanging off trees, as if carried there by birds.

Manong Jose Discusses How the Boy and His Strangeness Grew into His Name

To say that the boy was touched is one thing. And people say it often. So it becomes many things. For example, a plant with an exceptional flower becomes a *tiger lily*.

Fidelito was like that. The world around him was veiled; sadness hung from the rooftops, the weather vanes. He was many things and many different directions such as life gives.

Think of the name one is given as a road. A couple driving down the road gets lost and knocks on a cottage door. A man with a terrible temper answers, holding a glass of wine. He is curt and the couple fear him, though he offers a glass of wine to each as part of the fineness of things. And so it goes, getting lost—history forever improvising.

Despite failing eyesight, she looks up. She is tired from pouring over a history book. When she sees a pair of moth's wings, her cataracts make them Fidelito's tear-thick eyelashes from when he fell from a tree. And the shadows of moth-flight in the bald eye of the light bulb are her son, who drifts like a loose rag. They cause her to drop the book and feel wind from airborne pages. Now the moths rest and pose sayings to her in white quotation marks. There on the mural of trees with sepia branches, the insects grasp.

The book, fallen to her feet, says that you can tell a man is having an affair by the angle of his shoulders. Maria Elena thinks the angle of a moth's wings are the same: her son's slouched eyebrows in concern.

Now the home without a son is bare as a spoon. But the vines from his mouth-marks on her breast still ache.

Once, to Fidelito, the weight of everything was measured by the angle of his mother's arms. Too far and he starved, too close and his head hurt. The same was true for Maria Elena: too far and her world was full of sirens. His lips too close, and her aureolas felt like a hill of ants.

Ants, she remembers, are the riddle. Their lives are always full of them. In a dream, Maria Elena believes that five ants learn the secret to fire. They pour into the room like rain and torch the mural of trees. They are jealous gods.

Fidelito makes halos by soaking bundles of sticks in water for hours. That is the first thing. They must bend without breaking. He tests one to see whether it will snap when he applies steady pressure. He knows the time.

Taking three sticks, he weaves them in and out as he would the hair of his mother. Forming a ring, he ties the ends as they meet with string.

But that's not the last thing. Fidelito must make it his own, this loop he will wear about his head. He looks for anything: discarded shirts with the crust of sea salt from his father—he tears them into strips. He cuts the straps off the dress his mother wears when she is most beautiful. Loose feathers and dry flowers that after being dead for months stay pink; these are gathered from the yard. Now he threads these into the spaces between sticks. Only then can he wear this hat to church or school.

Grace is found in the early hours. For the aura, he parades through streets with his palms upturned to the sky. Inhales. Exhales. The head arched back so far the ground disappears, and the name, in meditation, opens in cold air like a parachute.

Fidelito Speaks of One Evening at the Turn of a Century but Mentions No Particular Century

I'll be lifted by a tune I'll hear.
My whispered song—the hymn
Of birds, their beaks like shaky
Styluses clacking their orbits to time.
Some want this interval to last
But the last track is lovely. Going back
Further I feel I've missed something: the choir
At the center of the earth? I remember wanting
To leave the schoolyard, hearing that call,
The whistle in the wind.
I may just love difficulty. Those notes
Coming to my ears, the chorus
Beyond them, I try to understand
These songs, their time.